Configuration Management and CMDB

ServiceNow Special Edition

by Lawrence Miller

Configuration Management and CMDB For Dummies®, ServiceNow Special Edition

Published by
John Wiley & Sons, Inc.
111 River St.
Hoboken, NJ 07030-5774
www.wiley.com

Copyright © 2019 by John Wiley & Sons, Inc., Hoboken, New Jersey

No part of this publication may be reproduced, stored in a retrieval system or transmitted in any form or by any means, electronic, mechanical, photocopying, recording, scanning or otherwise, except as permitted under Sections 107 or 108 of the 1976 United States Copyright Act, without the prior written permission of the Publisher. Requests to the Publisher for permission should be addressed to the Permissions Department, John Wiley & Sons, Inc., 111 River Street, Hoboken, NJ 07030, (201) 748-6011, fax (201) 748-6008, or online at http://www.wiley.com/go/permissions.

Trademarks: Wiley, For Dummies, the Dummies Man logo, The Dummies Way, Dummies.com, Making Everything Easier, and related trade dress are trademarks or registered trademarks of John Wiley & Sons, Inc. and/or its affiliates in the United States and other countries, and may not be used without written permission. All other trademarks are the property of their respective owners. John Wiley & Sons, Inc., is not associated with any product or vendor mentioned in this book.

LIMIT OF LIABILITY/DISCLAIMER OF WARRANTY: THE PUBLISHER AND THE AUTHOR MAKE NO REPRESENTATIONS OR WARRANTIES WITH RESPECT TO THE ACCURACY OR COMPLETENESS OF THE CONTENTS OF THIS WORK AND SPECIFICALLY DISCLAIM ALL WARRANTIES, INCLUDING WITHOUT LIMITATION WARRANTIES OF FITNESS FOR A PARTICULAR PURPOSE. NO WARRANTY MAY BE CREATED OR EXTENDED BY SALES OR PROMOTIONAL MATERIALS. THE ADVICE AND STRATEGIES CONTAINED HEREIN MAY NOT BE SUITABLE FOR EVERY SITUATION. THIS WORK IS SOLD WITH THE UNDERSTANDING THAT THE PUBLISHER IS NOT ENGAGED IN RENDERING LEGAL, ACCOUNTING, OR OTHER PROFESSIONAL SERVICES. IF PROFESSIONAL ASSISTANCE IS REQUIRED, THE SERVICES OF A COMPETENT PROFESSIONAL PERSON SHOULD BE SOUGHT. NEITHER THE PUBLISHER NOR THE AUTHOR SHALL BE LIABLE FOR DAMAGES ARISING HEREFROM. THE FACT THAT AN ORGANIZATION OR WEBSITE IS REFERRED TO IN THIS WORK AS A CITATION AND/OR A POTENTIAL SOURCE OF FURTHER INFORMATION DOES NOT MEAN THAT THE AUTHOR OR THE PUBLISHER ENDORSES THE INFORMATION THE ORGANIZATION OR WEBSITE MAY PROVIDE OR RECOMMENDATIONS IT MAY MAKE. FURTHER, READERS SHOULD BE AWARE THAT INTERNET WEBSITES LISTED IN THIS WORK MAY HAVE CHANGED OR DISAPPEARED BETWEEN WHEN THIS WORK WAS WRITTEN AND WHEN IT IS READ.

ISBN 978-1-119-59403-1 (pbk); ISBN 978-1-119-59409-3 (ebk)

Manufactured in the United States of America

10 9 8 7 6 5 4 3 2 1

For general information on our other products and services, or how to create a custom *For Dummies* book for your business or organization, please contact our Business Development Department in the U.S. at 877-409-4177, contact info@dummies.biz, or visit www.wiley.com/go/custompub. For information about licensing the *For Dummies* brand for products or services, contact BrandedRights&Licenses@Wiley.com.

Publisher's Acknowledgments

Some of the people who helped bring this book to market include the following:

Development Editor: Elizabeth Kuball

Copy Editor: Elizabeth Kuball

Acquisitions Editor: Katie Mohr

Editorial Manager: Rev Mengle

Business Development Representative: Karen Hattan

Production Editor: Mohammed Zafar Ali

Special Help: Michael Ludwig, Richard Brounstein, Aleck Lin, Lisa Wolfe, and Navin Sharma

Table of Contents

INTRODUCTION 1
    About This Book 1
    Foolish Assumptions 2
    Icons Used in This Book 2
    Beyond the Book 3
    Where to Go from Here 3

CHAPTER 1: Configuration Management 101 5
    Covering the Basics of Configuration Management 5
    Creating a Configuration Management Plan 7
        Setting your direction 7
        Building your team and a governance model 9
        Designing your configuration data model 11
        Operationalizing configuration management 12
        Creating ongoing strategic alignment 13

CHAPTER 2: Exploring Configuration Management Use Cases 15
    Incident, Problem, and Change Management 15
        Preventing business service outages 16
        Identifying and responding to service outages
        more quickly 17
        Diagnosing and fixing service outages faster 17
    Operations Management 18
    Asset Management 19
    Security Management 20
    Audit and Compliance 21

CHAPTER 3: Building the Configuration Management Database 25
    Understanding Configuration Items 25
    Creating a Services-Oriented View 28
    Populating the CMDB Manually and with
    Automated Technologies 28
    Chronicling the Configuration Item Life Cycle 30
    Exploring Configuration Management in
    a DevOps/Cloud World 32

CHAPTER 4: **Keeping the Configuration Management Database Healthy and Trusted** 35
  Addressing Configuration Management Database Issues 35
  Building Trust in the Configuration Management Team and the Data 39
  Measuring Success 40
  Leveraging the CMDB Health Dashboard 41

CHAPTER 5: **Ten Important Milestones on the Configuration Management Journey** 43

Introduction

With so much of the modern enterprise powered by IT, visibility into IT infrastructure is mission critical. This sought-after visibility, however, is remarkably elusive. IT infrastructure continues to grow and become more complex, especially with the proliferation of hardware, software, appliances, virtual machines, cloud services, and mobile devices. This makes visibility into infrastructure a moving target.

For IT to gain visibility, it faces the challenge of consolidating, maintaining, and understanding complex data. First, IT must consolidate disparate configuration item (CI) data into a single configuration management database (CMDB), considering unknown CIs, inconsistent data quality, and ill-defined relationships. Then IT has to regularly maintain this complex data for accuracy. Finally, IT must be able to make sense of this complex data to drive business decisions and services. In general, CMDB projects have a reputation for failed starts, lengthy implementations, and ongoing maintenance challenges — often resulting in limited business value and unrewarded effort.

Most organizations face difficult challenges when initially implementing a configuration management capability. In this book, you find out how to build and maintain an effective configuration management capability for your organization.

About This Book

Configuration Management For Dummies consists of five chapters that explore the following:

- >> The basics of configuration management (Chapter 1)
- >> Configuration management use cases (Chapter 2)
- >> How to build a configuration management database (Chapter 3)
- >> How to maintain a configuration management database (Chapter 4)
- >> Key milestones on your journey to configuration management (Chapter 5)

Foolish Assumptions

It's been said that most assumptions have outlived their uselessness, but I assume a few things nonetheless!

Mainly, I assume that you're an IT executive, director, manager, or administrator responsible for managing and supporting your organization's IT environment, including data center infrastructure, cloud systems, and end-user devices. As such, this book is written primarily for technical readers with at least a basic understanding of IT operations management.

If any of these assumptions describe you, then this book is for you! If none of these assumptions describe you, keep reading anyway. It's a great book and when you finish reading it, you'll know a few things about configuration management.

Icons Used in This Book

Throughout this book, I occasionally use special icons to call attention to important information. Here's what to expect:

REMEMBER

This icon points out information you should commit to your gray matter — along with anniversaries and birthdays!

TECHNICAL STUFF

If you seek to attain the seventh level of NERD-vana, perk up! This icon explains the jargon beneath the jargon!

TIP

Tips are appreciated, never expected — and I sure hope you'll appreciate these useful nuggets of information.

WARNING

These alerts point out the stuff your mother warned you about (well, probably not), but they do offer practical advice.

Beyond the Book

There's only so much I can cover in 48 short pages, so if you find yourself at the end of this book, thinking, "Where can I learn more?," just go to www.servicenow.com.

Where to Go from Here

If you don't know where you're going, any chapter will get you there — but Chapter 1 might be a good place to start! However, if you see a particular topic that piques your interest, feel free to jump ahead to that chapter. Each chapter is written to stand on its own, so you can read this book in any order that suits you (though I don't recommend upside down or backward).

IN THIS CHAPTER

» Defining configuration management

» Getting started with a configuration management plan

Chapter **1**
Configuration Management 101

In this chapter, you see what configuration management is all about and how to develop a plan to successfully implement configuration management in your organization.

Covering the Basics of Configuration Management

Your IT environment contains many different components. To deliver business services, these components need to be properly configured. Configuration management is the set of processes that manage these configuration activities. This includes recording configuration data, ensuring that configuration changes are appropriately authorized, and auditing to ensure that configuration data remains accurate. ITIL defines configuration management as:

> The process responsible for ensuring that assets required to deliver services are properly controlled, and that accurate and reliable information about those assets is available when and where it is needed. This information includes details of how the assets have been configured and the relationships between them.

Configuration management has its roots in the U.S. Department of Defense (DoD), where it emerged as a management discipline for hardware material items used on large military projects in the 1950s. Configuration management is defined in the U.S. military standard MIL-STD-3046 as the following:

> An engineering and management process [that] ensures [that] the configuration of an item is known and documented and changes to an item are controlled and tracked for purposes of establishing and maintaining consistency of a product's performance, functional, and physical attributes with its requirements, design, and operational information.

This definition emphasizes the underlying value proposition of configuration management: Ensure a product or service matches its documentation and meets expectations. The Institute of Configuration Management reports that having clear, complete, and concise information to manage your products and services, which comes from a configuration management capability, can reduce the cost of sales by up to 40 percent by reducing the need for corrective action.

Configuration management has become essential for enterprise IT and the services they provide. Large projects have failed because of a lack of configuration knowledge, and change management is nearly impossible without good configuration management. Poor change management is also the biggest culprit in service outages. Maintaining good configuration management standards and policies enables organizations to run more smoothly. Configuration management is also critical for corporate projects that involve technology to be successful. Some common examples include the following:

- Data center moves
- Data center reconciliation
- Development of a new strategic software product
- Corporate growth through mergers and acquisitions

WARNING

The concept of configuration management and the configuration management database (CMDB, discussed in Chapter 3) are different but often confused. The CMDB is analogous to the plumbing in your house and configuration management is the water quality.

Creating a Configuration Management Plan

Every successful CMDB deployment needs a detailed configuration management plan. When you clearly identify your objectives and develop a comprehensive strategy for designing, implementing, and sustaining your configuration management capability, you lay the foundation for greater business service health.

The following activities are key to a successful configuration management plan and CMDB deployment:

- Set your direction.
- Build your team and a governance model.
- Design your configuration data model.
- Operationalize configuration management.
- Create ongoing strategic alignment.

Setting your direction

Great configuration management starts with clear goals, actionable objectives, and measurable business outcomes. When you're setting goals and objectives, be sure to address the following questions:

- What do you want to accomplish?
- What is your approach and what are your constraints and assumptions?
- What business outcomes will your CMDB support?
- How do you know that you're on track?

Your CMDB needs to support your business and IT strategy. Start by identifying your company's key initiatives. These might include things such as the following:

- Digital transformation
- Business growth through acquisition

- » Expanding your customer base
- » Moving to subscription-based product licensing

Don't forget to include strategic initiatives within your IT department, such as:

- » Aligning IT with the business
- » Adopting a cloud-first strategy
- » Enhancing information security
- » Automation and machine learning
- » Implementing blockchain

TIP

When describing strategic business initiatives, use the same language that your company already uses. Your stakeholders will understand more quickly, and you'll get faster buy-in.

Next, create a list of use cases that support your strategic initiatives and how they tie back to the CMDB. Table 1-1 provides a few examples.

TABLE 1-1 Examples of Strategic Initiatives and Configuration Management Use Cases

Strategic Initiative	Use Case	How This Ties Back to the CMDB
Align IT with the business.	An IT component breaks. How do we know if this affects one of our mission-critical business services?	Create an accurate, up-to-date view of which infrastructure components support each of your critical business services.
Expand customer base.	We want to add new interactive services to our existing customer website. How do we ensure our website will continue to scale?	Track website infrastructure and applications to provide input for performance optimization and enterprise architecture evolution.

Strategic Initiative	Use Case	How This Ties Back to the CMDB
Improve information security.	We need to ensure compliance with the Payment Card Industry Data Security Standards (PCI DSS). Which parts of our infrastructure do we need to protect and audit?	Add CI attributes to indicate which IT components store or have access to customer credit card information.
Implement a cloud-first strategy.	We're going to migrate our inventory control system to the cloud. How do we plan this migration?	Identify all the inventory control system components that need to be migrated by creating a service map.

You need to develop a road map and scope for meeting your configuration management plan objectives that includes short-term goals with measurable results. For example, "All hardware assets will be accurately tracked by March 31 in phase 1."

Finally, develop a training plan for your users and a communication plan to ensure the configuration management team receives important communications (for example, about new technology initiatives).

Building your team and a governance model

When you build your configuration management team and governance structure and get early buy-in from executives, it helps create credibility and trust in your configuration management process over the long term.

The configuration management team should have autonomy to carry out configuration management responsibilities without being bogged down by daily support functions. This team should operate independently from the day-to-day "keep the lights on" support functions.

With your team in place, define and document each member's role, responsibilities, and authority to ensure they have the ownership and support to make the changes required.

Table 1-2 shows examples of some typical roles and responsibilities for a configuration management team.

TABLE 1-2 Typical Assignments for a Configuration Management Team

Role	Responsibility	Title
Configuration management executive sponsor Configuration control board (CCB) process owner	Oversees configuration management plan implementation in all departments within the company	Senior executive
Configuration management process owner CCB chair	Has ownership and is accountable for its strategic development Ensures configuration management plan is rolled out	Senior manager
Configuration manager (full CCB member/guest member)	Manages delivery of configuration management services and documentation of operating procedures	IT manager
Configuration management system analyst (full CCB member/guest member)	Performs daily configuration management tasks with minimal direction	IT analyst
Configuration management specialist (full CCB member/guest member)	Performs daily configuration management tasks with direction from configuration management system analyst	IT admin

As part of the configuration management team, you should form a CCB to implement governance. The CCB is essential and is there to oversee your configuration management program, making sure that it delivers value, stays on track, and operates effectively. Voting members of your CCB should be leadership team members who are directly accountable for the strategic initiatives of the IT department and close enough to the day-to-day infrastructure support team efforts to understand the use cases.

You need to determine what configuration management policies already exist in your organization, if they're still relevant and effective, and what additional policies may need to be created.

Designing your configuration data model

Now, it's time to decide what data you're going to keep in your CMDB. You do this by defining which configuration item (CI) classes you need.

TECHNICAL STUFF

A CI is one of the most important components of your CMDB. It's simply an application, infrastructure, or service component you're managing. It can be a physical server, an app running on a virtual server, or a business service, among others. You can find out more about CIs in Chapter 3.

Before you start, familiarize yourself with the CMDB and its capabilities and features. Develop an understanding of the design options for the CMDB and the broader ecosystem of federated systems and data feeds.

Trying to build a comprehensive CMDB right away is a mistake. Start simply and then make incremental improvements as your configuration management capabilities mature. Decide which CI classes and attributes you need to support the data needs of the use cases you identified earlier. If you find yourself defining CI classes or attributes that aren't needed for these use cases, you're off track.

For example, you might start with a hardware CI class, so you assign some simple attributes: CPU, memory, and so on. As you build your CMDB, you'll map computers, servers, routers, switches, and other hardware. Each of these CIs will have attributes, and each of them will have relationships and dependencies. By taking this approach, you can launch basic capabilities quickly, and then introduce additional CI classes over time as you grow your capabilities and scope (see Figure 1-1).

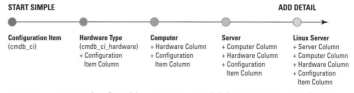

FIGURE 1-1: Example of a table extension model that grows in complexity.

WARNING

Your CI tables can get out of control quickly if you don't simplify them. Keep their names intuitive so they're easy to identify and remember.

WARNING

For your configuration data model, only focus on the CIs that are necessary to meet the use cases your users require. There are many CI classes that are populated automatically by discovery tools that you don't need to focus on (for example, "Next Hop Routing Rules" of network devices). If you don't need this data to satisfy use cases for any processes or reporting, then these classes don't need to be in your data dictionary, and you shouldn't waste your time verifying that they're correct.

Operationalizing configuration management

Now that you have your configuration data model, it's time to get your CMDB up and running. However, creating a healthy CMDB isn't a one-time activity. To maintain a healthy CMDB, you need to put processes and tools in place to keep your CMDB up to date and accurate — and you need to document these in your configuration management plan. This work needs to be done continuously; otherwise, your CMDB will fall into disrepair and all your hard work will be lost.

Think about questions such as the following:

- What information — for example, operational status — do stakeholders need for each CI?
- How do you ensure that this information is clear, concise, and valid?
- Which CIs can you keep up to date automatically?
- Which CIs have to be updated manually, and who is responsible for this?
- How do you control changes in your CMDB?
- How do you monitor the health of your CMDB?

Effective change management is critical for a healthy CMDB. Uncontrolled change creates risks, breaks configuration management processes, and creates an unreliable CMDB. For example, if someone incorrectly marks a server as out-of-service, this could ultimately lead to a service outage.

To avoid this, do the following:

- » Use a change management system to handle change requests.
- » Ensure that changes are reviewed and approved before they're made, and utilize process automation to gain velocity.
- » Configure permissions so that only authorized users can make changes to your CMDB.
- » Communicate changes to stakeholders.

Creating ongoing strategic alignment

A configuration management plan is a living document. Your business isn't standing still, and neither can your plan. It needs to stay aligned with business strategy and respond to new business initiatives. Effective two-way communication with business stakeholders is critical so that you understand their needs and they understand how you plan to support them.

Leverage your CCB to drive this alignment. This is where you can prioritize and evolve your configuration management road map to maximize the benefits for your business. By providing leadership and managerial oversight, your CCB should create a forum for effective decision-making — turning the discipline of configuration management into a high-value asset for your business.

Also, tailor your configuration management plan to align with major projects. Assign a configuration management team resource to each strategic project, so they understand how it impacts configuration management. For example, think about the first project in your business that uses containers. The last thing you want is a request for new CI classes two days before you go live.

> **IN THIS CHAPTER**
> » Accelerating IT service management
> » Creating a single source of truth for IT operations management
> » Keeping track of organizational IT assets
> » Improving information security
> » Supporting audit and compliance requirements

Chapter 2
Exploring Configuration Management Use Cases

In this chapter, I show you some common use cases for configuration management.

Incident, Problem, and Change Management

Incident management, problem management, and change management are core functions in IT service management (ITSM). The configuration management database (CMDB) consolidates disparate IT management systems into a single system of action, allowing IT to see exactly what assets are in your IT environment, what services they're related to, and how they're functioning at all times.

The service desk can quickly see the relationship between configuration items (CIs) and services to resolve incidents and problems. Incident management mapping directly improves the service desk readiness to resolve issues faster. When this mapping is in place, both IT and business partners are on the same page about tracking issues in impacted services, which significantly improves mean time to resolution (MTTR). Similarly, the change advisory board (CAB) can proactively manage the impact of changes on your services.

TIP

Find and address potential failure points by periodically reviewing CI relationship maps and ensuring CMDB accuracy.

A healthy CMDB empowers ITSM and increases business service quality by helping you to

- Prevent business service outages.
- Identify and respond to service outages more quickly.
- Diagnose and fix service outages faster.

Preventing business service outages

An ounce of prevention is worth a pound of cure. That's why stopping business service outages before they start is so important. Not only does this improve service availability, but it also reduces the run-rate workload for IT operations teams — freeing up time for strategic initiatives and further service improvements.

Changes are one of the major causes of service outages. Unless you understand how a change affects your IT infrastructure and business services, there's a good chance it will cause an outage. A healthy CMDB lets you understand this impact.

For example, think about upgrading a software component in your infrastructure. How do you know which other software components this interacts with — and whether these are compatible with the new upgrade? Can the component be upgraded in isolation, or do multiple components need to be upgraded as part of a cascading change? With a healthy CMDB, you can understand the relationships between software components, and you can also see the version of each component. This means you can plan the upgrade correctly, eliminating the risk of unanticipated outages.

Service maps take this to the next level. Now, you can accurately assess the impact of infrastructure changes on complete business services. For instance, assume that you need to take an infrastructure component offline temporarily. What business services does this impact? If you don't know, you risk creating a service outage. With service maps, you know which business services are affected and can plan accordingly — for instance, by executing the change during a planned business service maintenance window.

Identifying and responding to service outages more quickly

IT operations teams spend huge amounts of time trying to make sense of events from their monitoring systems. First, the sheer volume is overwhelming, particularly when you're dealing with thousands and thousands of event notifications. Second, most monitoring systems typically give you an isolated view of your infrastructure or application — there is no easy way to see which business services are affected. Often, the first time that IT operations knows about a business service outage is when end users complain.

By integrating an event management platform with your CMDB, you can tackle this problem head-on. Event management deduplicates and filters events across all your monitoring systems, turning a flood of events into a trickle of meaningful alerts. It binds these alerts to corresponding CIs in your CMDB, so you know which IT components are affected — and who is responsible for diagnosing and fixing them.

But that's just the start. Event management also correlates events using service maps in the CMDB to determine the health of your business services. This determination is made by assessing the impact from events in the context of CI dependencies. You get a service health dashboard that shows you the real-time health of all your business services. You can see at a glance when there is a service issue, and you can prioritize your response, so you focus on your most critical business services. The result? You cut through the infrastructure noise, identifying and responding to service outages more quickly and intelligently.

Diagnosing and fixing service outages faster

How does a healthy CMDB help you to diagnose and fix service outages faster?

Event management (discussed in the preceding section) does more than provide a service health dashboard. It also lets you drill down into the underlying service map, automatically showing which CIs are experiencing issues. This makes diagnosing service outages much simpler because you can see how issues are propagating across the business service. For instance, if an application monitoring system is reporting slow response times, you can easily correlate this back to the underlying cause — such as an overloaded virtual machine or a failed high-capacity network link.

Using this service map, you can also identify historical activity that could have caused the business service outage. For example, you can easily see which CIs have recently been reconfigured, which ones have recently undergone change management, or which ones have had incidents leading up to the outage. Again, this helps you to pinpoint likely causes of outages, dramatically accelerating diagnosis and reducing mean time to resolution (MTTR).

You can also configure remediation actions and trigger them either manually by clicking a CI on the service map, or automatically by defining trigger conditions. For example, this might include automatically collecting logs from a server, freeing up additional disk space, or restarting an application. By linking these actions to CIs, you don't just diagnose service outages faster — you fix them faster.

Operations Management

IT operations management (ITOM) consists of the day-to-day administrative tasks and processes necessary to monitor and control IT infrastructure and services.

The worlds of ITSM (discussed earlier in this chapter) and ITOM are commonly separate today within the wider IT organization. ITSM personnel are typically service-oriented, while ITOM personnel are infrastructure-oriented.

At a minimum, there's a language barrier. But the more common reality is that other barriers affect the combined effectiveness of both worlds, including the following:

- » A different focus and understanding of what's important
- » Different objectives and performance metrics (and both sets may also be disconnected from higher-level business objectives)
- » A level of operational and management disconnectedness that — at a minimum — delays the other party in delivering against business needs

Organizations need to bring service management and operations management together so that they can work together for better IT and business outcomes. Establishing a single system of record — the CMDB — is an important first step.

Creating and populating a CMDB — even if you're just starting with network assets and a few services — provides your organization with a strategic advantage by connecting many aspects of your business. With the CMDB in place, your organization will have a single source of truth across all of IT. The CMDB allows operations management and service management staff to work together better on incident and event management, resulting in fewer and less damaging IT issues.

REMEMBER

The CMDB provides a platform for a wider spectrum of ITSM and ITOM capabilities that contribute to better business outcomes — for example:

» The ability to map monitoring alerts to the services affected to better understand their impact

» Improved compliance and cost optimization activities

» Enhanced change and release assessment, planning, and delivery

Asset Management

Asset management is usually considered a financial function where information for certain items is managed and reported. IT departments usually support this effort by providing information about the status, location, and management of IT components to the finance department.

A configuration management platform can be used to track physical (hardware) assets, software assets (licensing), and consumables (items often below the asset threshold value but widely needed throughout the business).

Configuration management depends on a solid set of basic asset management functions. New IT hardware must first be requested, approved, ordered, and received before the IT department deploys it into an operational state where it becomes a CI.

Figure 2-1 illustrates that some items are just assets (chairs, desks, artwork, and so on) and some things are just CIs (business services, virtual servers, and so on). Some items (routers, physical servers, laptops, and so on) are both assets and CIs.

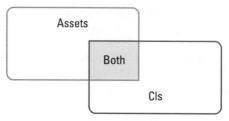

FIGURE 2-1: Asset and CI overlap.

To illustrate this concept, consider this question: Is a printer a CI, an asset, or both? The average personal desktop printer is pretty inexpensive nowadays — likely to be under your organizational financial threshold for an asset. So, chances are, a personal desktop printer would be classified as a consumable rather than an asset.

A magnetic ink character recognition (MICR) printer in the finance department that is used to print checks that are mailed to customers, print paychecks, and so on would be treated as both an asset and a CI. Key business services are dependent on that printer and if the printer is broken, those related services are impacted.

Now, consider the network printer at the end of the hall which serves your entire office floor. If it isn't leased, in all probability it has a value over your organization's financial threshold, making it an asset. But is it a CI? Is any business service dependent upon that printer to deliver services? In all likelihood, no, because there is always the option to use another nearby printer for people to accomplish their work. So, this printer is just an asset. When the printer needs maintenance or changes, it's handled through a service request rather than change management.

Security Management

A single source of truth — the CMDB — is likewise a valuable tool for security management teams. The CMDB offers easy access to data, which is useful to security management. When a security incident occurs, the affected assets can be matched against the CMDB to determine priority based on how critical the asset is to your business.

Security teams can leverage the CMDB to map threats, security incidents, and vulnerabilities to business services along with IT infrastructure. Business service mappings in the CMDB help security management teams to quickly assess the nature and scope of a breach or potential threat so that response and remediation efforts can be appropriately prioritized. This mapping enables prioritization and risk scoring based on business impact, ensuring your security teams are focused on what is most critical to your business. Working in a single platform also makes handing off tasks to IT simple and adds the benefits of visibility, service-level agreement (SLA) tracking, and live collaboration tools.

The CMDB also enables the security management team to proactively manage vulnerabilities within the IT environment by identifying firmware, operating system, and software versions installed on CIs, as well as current patch levels.

Misconfigured software can leave an organization open to attackers in much the same way as vulnerabilities. These configuration issues include incorrect permissions, weak passwords, access controls, and more. An organization sets policies to define secure configurations (for example, minimum password-length requirements), and then runs a scan using a security configuration assessment tool to test assets against these policies to find any misconfigured assets. Next, failed configuration test results are matched against assets in the CMDB. Data from the CMDB determines how important each asset is to the business, and that business criticality is one factor in the risk score used to prioritize failed results.

TIP

You should also consult with your information security team to have them assess the risks and vulnerabilities of having sensitive data (such as IP addresses, connection protocols, current patch levels, support staff names and phone numbers, and so on) available to all staff who will be using the CMDB.

Audit and Compliance

Practically every organization in every industry today is subject to various regulatory requirements. Some examples include

- **》 Sarbanes-Oxley Act of 2002 (SOX):** Applicable to publicly traded companies
- **》 Health Insurance Portability and Accountability Act of 1996 (HIPAA):** Applicable to healthcare providers and insurers

> **Payment Card Industry Data Security Standard (PCI DSS):** Applicable to any organization that stores or processes payment card (such as credit card or debit card) information

Additionally, many organizations are subject to federal government regulations and certification programs.

Although these various regulations differ in their requirements, they all share the common goal of ensuring that sensitive data and systems are appropriately secured and proper governance and accountability is established. Configuration management and change management controls are often specifically required to achieve and maintain compliance.

The CMDB is an essential tool to help organizations meet their audit and compliance needs. Audits may be required by outside entities or may be an internal requirement. For some organizations, an outside regulatory body may require regular proof that a company is meeting certain IT standards or maintaining certain information. Meeting the needs of the auditors is more than just a matter of a filing requirement. A corporation can face serious financial penalties, slow their ability to run the business, be susceptible to dangerous security threats, or even lose their license to operate in an industry. That's why any company must take audits very seriously and make sure they're completed in the most accurate and efficient manner possible. Having an accurate CMDB can help greatly here. Audits usually fall into two categories:

> **Legal compliance** that is required by a regulatory body (for example, SOX, which is required by the U.S. Securities and Exchange Commission, and HIPAA, required by the U.S. Department of Health and Human Services)

> **Internal corporate needs** as required by departments to help satisfy internal processes

As with all use cases for the CMDB, the configuration management team should be leveraged to ensure the CMDB will meet the compliance use cases. This is necessary so that the configuration team can ensure that the data needed for the audit reports exists in the CMDB, and also so that the configuration team can ensure that the data is complete and accurate. Here are some examples of audit reports where an accurate CMDB can be leveraged:

» Report on each infrastructure component, including network devices, software applications, and desktop computers that comprise each high priority business service for the organization.

» Report on each production server for each business service for an organization. In addition, provide the name of the failover server for each server in production.

» Report on the physical servers supporting each node of a high-availability cluster. Ensure that different physical servers are used for each redundant node so that there is no single point of failure.

» Report on each major software application, with version and patch level to ensure that they're running the latest security patches and that no system is falling behind, to reduce the security risk.

> **IN THIS CHAPTER**
> - » Defining configuration item components
> - » Recognizing the value of a services-oriented view
> - » Populating the database
> - » Managing configuration items throughout their life cycles
> - » Assessing challenges and opportunities in DevOps and cloud environments

Chapter 3
Building the Configuration Management Database

In this chapter, you find out how to build a configuration management database (CMDB), including creating configuration items (CIs), adopting a services-oriented view, populating the CMDB, maintaining CIs throughout their life cycles, and adapting your CMDB in a DevOps and cloud world.

Understanding Configuration Items

A CMDB is a purpose-built database for configuration management. The fundamental building block of a CMDB is the CI. A CI represents an item under configuration management, such as a router, a server, an application, or even a logical construct such as a portfolio.

Each CI in the CMDB must have at least one unique identifier that does not change for the life of the CI. This concept may seem simple in theory, but it can be challenging to implement and needs to be well thought out for each CI class that you will be implementing. For example, if an organization deploys PCs with the same host name without other unique identifying attributes such as a serial number, a single CI will be incorrectly created to represent multiple PCs. Likewise, if the IP address of a device is used as the primary CI identifier, multiple CIs could be incorrectly created for the same device if the IP address changes.

Each CI has attributes that describe the component. For instance, a server CI may have CPU, memory, and other attributes. Table 3-1 contains some other examples of possible CI attributes.

TABLE 3-1 Examples of CI Classes and Attributes

CI Classes	CI Attributes
Application	Build Code version Code language Compiler version Source code repository location
Hardware	Hostname CPU Memory IP address MAC address Manufacturer Model Operating system version Serial number Firmware version
Facilities	Facilities contact Geographic region Physical address
Reference data	Client ID Location ID Organizational ID Physical address

Information about CIs frequently comes from multiple data sources. These data sources may provide overlapping information for the same attributes and CIs as other discovery sources. The best solution for this problem is to use a configuration management platform that has the capability to rank how information will be used from multiple overlapping sources of data. If you do not have this capability available to you, then the CMDB manager must designate a single source of truth for each attribute of each CI type and only allow that data source to make changes to that attribute. In this case, there should be only a single source of truth for any attribute of any CI; otherwise, the CI could be marked as changed with attributes flip-flopping on a regular basis when no real changes were actually made (see Figure 3-1).

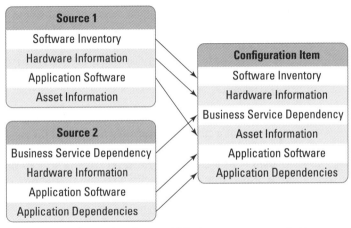

FIGURE 3-1: Attribute values from multiple data sources reconciled to a single source of truth for a CI.

CIs also have relationships, and these are stored in the CMDB as well. For example, a server may interface with a specific router, so the server has a relationship with that router. Relationships are very useful because they show how your IT infrastructure is connected, which helps you do things such as impact analysis in change planning, root cause analysis in diagnosing outages, and service architecture optimization.

REMEMBER

A CMDB doesn't just contain information about your IT environment. It also puts business context around it. For example, it shows which person or organization owns each CI and is responsible for maintaining it. This is just one example — CIs can have

CHAPTER 3 **Building the Configuration Management Database** 27 many business-oriented attributes that help you to manage CIs and related business services.

Creating a Services-Oriented View

Traditionally, IT has managed IT infrastructure. However, this is changing rapidly. Businesses don't care about servers or routers. They care about the critical business services they use to run operations, engage customers, drive revenues, increase efficiency, and create new business insights. Rather than focusing on infrastructure, IT must ensure that these business services are highly available, responsive, and cost-effective.

To do this, you have to know how these business services are delivered. Service maps give you this visibility. They show you which CIs support a particular business service and how these CIs are related. These service maps are derived from CIs held directly in your CMDB, connecting your business services to your infrastructure.

Here's a simple analogy to help you understand service maps. Think about a city road map, showing you all the roads in the city and where they intersect. This is the equivalent of CIs and relationships in your CMDB. However, this is still an infrastructure view. Now, think about a city bus map that shows different bus routes. These bus routes are like business service maps — they show the specific roads each route follows.

Why does this matter? What if there were an accident on a road? If you just had a road map, you wouldn't know which bus routes were affected. For that, you need a bus map. Similarly, if a web server fails in your IT environment, how do you know which business services are affected? You need a service map — the infrastructure view alone doesn't give you the answer.

Populating the CMDB Manually and with Automated Technologies

Manually entering information about CIs is time-consuming and can be error-prone. Even in a small organization, too many changes take place and manual entry cannot be depended on for very long. Yet, many organizations start out using this method to establish their CMDB before automated processes are created.

Automated technologies that can discover CIs are the most efficient, repeatable, and accurate method for populating the CMDB. Mature, automated solutions, such as ServiceNow Discovery and Service Mapping, can automatically discover entities and relationships across applications, servers, databases, storage, and networking devices to give visibility into an entire infrastructure stack — for both traditional and cloud infrastructure. Mature automated technologies also can map the relationship between business services and underlying infrastructure. In general, look for automated technologies that can accomplish three key tasks:

» **Application service mapping:** The most reliable method for discovering the relationship between infrastructure and business services is using automated business service mapping. This involves scanning the business application from an entry point and tracing the application flow from one server to the next until all the dependent servers and software components are mapped. During this scan, configuration information is read to understand application dependencies. A business service mapping approach should be used when business application CIs need to be tracked.

» **Infrastructure discovery:** Automated infrastructure discovery scans IP addresses in the organization's network at a regularly scheduled interval. For each IP address discovered, the automated process logs into the device and collects hardware and software information. An infrastructure discovery approach — customized as necessary to collect the correct CIs — effectively gathers an accurate inventory of every device in the organization.

» **Cloud discovery:** Automated cloud resource discovery to gain visibility into private or public cloud resources (such as VMware, Amazon Web Services, Microsoft Azure, Google Cloud, and IBM Cloud), by leveraging API calls to the respective provider, along with their relationships and dependencies and update the CMDB.

Some data cannot be gathered automatically, such as business and organizational information. Information about people cannot be gathered by a scan of the network and must be entered either manually or via Lightweight Directory Access Protocol (LDAP) or a direct integration with your human resources system. Some other examples of attributes that must be manually entered or integrated from other reference systems include

- >> Data center location
- >> Floor and room number
- >> Rack location
- >> Department owner
- >> Asset tag
- >> Business unit
- >> Organizational unit

So, for most organizations a combination of manual and automated processes is needed to populate and maintain the CMDB.

TIP

Information entered manually doesn't necessarily have to be entered by the CMDB manager. Processes can be established that require employees to enter information about data center resources for which they're responsible. For example, an employee or a department owner can fill out an asset request through an automated service catalog and have many of the manual fields required for the CMDB for that configuration item already populated.

Finally, external data sources often contain information that needs to be populated into the CMDB. These data sources are usually established internal databases that are already maintained by the organization, or a vendor-supplied database with configuration information that is relevant to the CMDB. If the information in the external source is static, a one-time import of the data to the CMDB is all that is necessary. More often the data will change, and a regular feed will be needed to copy the relevant configuration data over to the CMDB.

Chronicling the Configuration Item Life Cycle

From the time of its creation to the time that it's no longer needed, a CI will typically transition through several operational states (for example, "Operational," "Repair in Progress," and

"Retired"). These operational states have no bearing on the existence of the CI and merely indicate its current status, very much akin to traditional asset management practices. The important thing to note here is that CIs should never be deleted because this has ramifications not only from an audit compliance perspective, but also in terms of records associated with the CI, such as incidents that have occurred and the history of changes that have been implemented over the life cycle of the CI.

The true life cycle of a CI begins at the time someone makes the request for that CI to exist. This could be a purchase request for a piece of hardware or software that will be delivered and set up, or it could be a request for a virtual machine to be instantiated in a private or public cloud environment. It is at this time that the CI can exist, even though no actual technology is running in the data center. The machine may still be in the box in the shipping/receiving office. Its status at this time could be "On order" or "Pending install." The CI may have many different statuses in its life cycle that go beyond operational states, for example:

- In stock
- Installed
- Pending repair
- Maintenance
- Absent
- Retired
- Donated
- Stolen
- Any other status that makes sense to track for the organization's asset life cycle needs

In addition, a CI, once retired may come out of retirement, if necessary. A CI may also change class completely. It may have been running a Microsoft Windows operating system, then be converted to a Linux operating system while still being the same CI. What's important for the CI is that its unique attributes (for example, serial number) used for identification remain the same. Tracking the history of the CI will give the organization great value in optimizing assets and meeting compliance needs.

Exploring Configuration Management in a DevOps/Cloud World

The advancement of technological capabilities and the tearing down of once-siloed IT disciplines in a DevOps, cloud-native world can make the role of configuration management a little, well, cloudy.

REMEMBER

DevOps — as its name implies — combines two previously siloed IT groups: the *developers* who build the applications and the *operations* groups who deploy and maintain them. In a DevOps environment, these two groups work together to accelerate and improve service delivery.

Continuous testing and continuous deployment are two DevOps practices that are key to the principle of "shifting left," in which teams focus on quality and begin testing much earlier in the software development life cycle. In this way, problems are detected and rectified in the lower release environments prior to deployment into production. Controlling the versioning of a compiled application to maintain continuity across release environments is relatively easy, but the infrastructure the application is deployed on across release environments is an entirely different story.

Automation tools commonly used to prepare infrastructure in DevOps environments still produce variances in infrastructure configurations. This results in servers that should share a common set of configurations being different, thus creating problems with applications functioning as designed. A configuration management database that can ingest data from across the DevOps tool chain provides the ability to compare and highlight infrastructure configuration differences across release environments over time. This capability will provide tremendous value to the DevOps goal of detecting problems in lower release environments and will also play a significant role in the meantime to resolution (MTTR) of incidents involving applications that have already been deployed into production.

Along with DevOps, several relatively new resources — often referred to as cloud-native technologies — are used to build applications in a service-oriented architecture (SOA). Cloud-native applications use cloud computing frameworks that are composed of loosely coupled cloud services. In this way, developers can break down tasks into separate services that can be executed across multiple servers.

These newer cloud-based frameworks can cause some confusion around what is or isn't a CI and how to source the metadata describing a CI. From a strict configuration management perspective, you must have the ability to change the configuration of a CI at some point during its life cycle for it to be considered a CI.

For bare-metal infrastructure, this concept is easily understood, as in the case of a server. Over the course of its life cycle, elements of a server's configuration — such as its operating system, its CPU, its IP address, and so on — can change. Even infrastructure that has been virtualized can have configuration changes made over their life cycles.

Now, let's consider some cloud-native technologies. Serverless computing, such as Function as a Service (FaaS), is a good place to start. The FaaS itself is a CI, with the name of the function as its primary identifier. It's also important to capture the code version of the function, as well as its memory footprint, which is usually the billing metric. The ephemeral nature of the execution of the function — which could last only microseconds — makes traditional discovery of the executing function challenging, but this has no bearing on its legitimacy as a CI. The ephemeral nature of the function is tied to its execution, not its life cycle, and its version and memory footprint can change over the course of its life cycle as part of an application. Because it may not be possible to capture the necessary metadata describing the function via traditional discovery tooling, it will be important to capture this information from the DevOps pipeline or by querying the cloud provider's application programming interface (API) post-deployment.

Next, let's look at a containerized environment executing via Kubernetes. The genesis (that is, originally deployed) containers are CIs, because their contents can be updated over time. The pods that hold the containers are also CIs, because they could be added to or reorganized over time. The Kubernetes orchestration layer is also a CI, because its parameters will determine how the application auto-scales on demand. Now comes the tricky part: What about the additional containers and pods (or possibly even clusters) that may be created through horizontal and vertical scaling based on the auto-scaling parameters defined in the orchestration layer? These additional containers and the pods that hold them are exact clones of the genesis containers and pods and will only exist temporarily during periods of increased demand for the application. These containers and pods cannot be changed because they're only replicas of the genesis items; under a strict configuration management interpretation, they would not be considered CIs themselves. However, these additional containers and pods are important. They need to be monitored via application performance monitoring and may trigger event streams that need to be correlated to incidents. Thus, they should be treated as CIs nonetheless.

Look for a configuration management platform that has the capability to regularly poll for or receive a push from cloud resources, to automatically create CIs for them, and manage their life cycles as appropriate.

In a DevOps cloud-native world, regardless of the technologies leveraged or the location of the infrastructure, an organization must still:

» Maintain governance over the applications and infrastructure providing services to the business. This means you must still have a record of who owns, manages, and supports the CIs in the service delivery chain.

» Be able to evaluate the risks involved in the delivery of services to the business (for example, evaluating the risks involved with changes to CIs that are actively involved in the delivery of services).

» Maintain the necessary controls to meet internal and regulatory compliance auditing requirements. These requirements vary by industry but commonly include tracking CIs that utilize or support controlled information such as personally identifiable information (PII), protected health information (PHI), or financial data, and a process that supports an approval workflow for proposed changes to CIs involved in the delivery of core services.

> **IN THIS CHAPTER**
> » Identifying and correcting data quality issues
> » Getting back on track when things go wrong
> » Creating a performance scorecard with objective metrics
> » Visualizing configuration management database health with a dashboard

Chapter 4
Keeping the Configuration Management Database Healthy and Trusted

Most organizations face difficult challenges when implementing a configuration management capability for the first time. In this chapter, you learn how to avoid some common configuration management database (CMDB) pitfalls, build trust in your team and the CMDB, measure success, and monitor the health of your CMDB.

Addressing Configuration Management Database Issues

A configuration item (CI) is the fundamental structural management unit of the CMDB, and it serves as the basis for the language for effective communication within your IT organization.

Everything IT supports is ultimately expressed in terms of CIs: Incidents are expressed in terms of degraded CI(s), problems are expressed in terms of which CIs are root causes and are impacted, changes are expressed in terms of which CIs are changing or are potentially impacted or at risk for a specific change, and so on.

Thus, the quality of CI data will be an essential tenet of your ability to effectively communicate the current state of items powering your services. As you work to define your CIs, you can initially expect to capture CI data from the data sources your organization has readily available. Most organizations find their current data may or may not be clear, concise, or complete — it is almost always of inconsistent quality. However, at some point during their initial implementation of a CMDB, most organizations decide to load their CMDBs with the best data available and embark on an ongoing effort to steadily improve data quality over time.

TIP

The configuration management team should be relentless in challenging the IT organization to improve CI data quality. You need to put technology and processes in place to ensure that the data within your CMDB remains accurate.

WARNING

Despite the best laid plans and advanced automation technologies, data quality problems will still inevitably arise. The most common problems found in a CMDB include

» **Incompletely populated CIs:** Automated discovery of CIs is the most efficient and effective manner for populating the CMDB, but not all information about a CI can be captured by automated technologies. Some examples may include a building, floor, or room number; a rack location; or an application owner's name and contact information. This type of information will need to be manually populated or imported via an integration and maintained in the CMDB.

» **Duplicate CIs:** If the identification rules for CIs do not ensure that each CI is uniquely expressed with identifiers that don't change, then duplicates of the same CI will appear in the CMDB. This data must be cleaned up and the identification rules and processes modified as necessary in order to ensure that this problem doesn't occur again. Duplicate CIs may also be in the CMDB, which may not be prevented or detected by good identification rules. Many times, duplicate CIs will manifest because of processes that are not controlled.

For example, a person may be manually entering CIs into the CMDB and not following established procedures. Because duplicates can and probably will happen, it's important for the configuration management team to actively look for duplicates in creative ways. Scanning the list of computers for duplicate names is a good idea to help find duplicate CIs. Also, looking for CIs that are missing common attributes such as serial numbers, names, hardware information, and other items populated through an automated mechanism is a good idea. If this data is not being populated, it increases the risk that duplicate CIs are being created.

» **Overloaded CIs:** An opposite problem of duplicate CIs exists when different CIs are identified as the same CI and one CI is created when several CIs should've been created. This is particularly problematic with virtual CIs and can indicate a problem with the identification rules and processes that must be handled as soon as possible to fix the CI data in the CMDB. This problem will manifest itself when reports or processes fail to list the CIs that the users know exist. An investigation by the configuration manager should reveal the source of the issue, which is most commonly an issue with identification rules.

» **Stale CIs:** A CI becomes stale when its existence has not been verified for a determined period of time. This could be one or two weeks for a host or network device. It could be as little as a few days for a network dependency connection. A CI may become stale in the CMDB because it has been physically removed from the network and, thus, can no longer be found by automated discovery processes. The CI may still exist, but it may be damaged or intentionally taken off the network. In any case, the CMDB manager must investigate the situation with all concerned parties and initiate a fix either to the CMDB in terms of proper status or to the hosts on the network.

» **Orphaned CIs:** These are CIs that don't relate to anything or you don't know why they exist. CIs can appear in the CMDB that are not well identified. These orphan CIs have no relationships with other CIs. This can be an indication of an issue with the import data source not being well defined, or an issue with the system that incorrectly removes relationships between CIs.

How do you address the challenge of keeping the CMDB healthy?

Preventing bad data is your first line of defense. This involves creating identification rules for CI and attribute population and reviewing every automation method that updates the CMDB. Make no assumptions that the data is correct.

The second line of defense is having regular reports run of the data looking for CI issues and bringing them to the attention of the configuration management team. A CMDB health dashboard (discussed later in this chapter) works well for this purpose.

Finally, regular data quality procedures must be implemented to look for defective data. These can exist as automated scripts that scan records in the CMDB to look for duplicates or other CI records with bad or incomplete data. This is a creative process that may

» Run a script that scans a table of records to look for two CIs of a class that have the same name and could be duplicates.

» Scan CIs for relationships that need to exist to assess records.

» Look at core attributes that are missing from CIs and create a workflow to resolve the issue.

An open channel must also exist between the users and the configuration management team to communicate defective CI data. A process (preferably automated) must exist to handle such defects. Most important, you don't want to just fix the defects — you need to fix the process that allowed the defects to occur in the first place.

TIP

Your end users should be a part of the quality control process if it doesn't take up too much of their time. Generally speaking,

» If you ask for something that takes less than 15 minutes, it will probably get done right away.

» If you ask for something that takes an hour, it will take a few days before it gets done.

» If you ask for something that takes more than an hour, it will probably never get done!

In quality assurance, when there are millions of possible permutations of tests you can run against software, it is impossible to run every permutation. Instead, you select test cases from different areas that will test a diverse enough range of functionality and give you the best chance of finding the defects, if they exist.

You can apply this thinking to doing quality assurance on your CMDB with less effort, even if you have millions of CIs. You don't need to manually verify every CI. You can identify a smaller set of CIs from different types in your data center. Example CI classes from which you might choose would include

- » Linux servers
- » Windows servers running on-premises
- » Windows servers running in Amazon Web Services (AWS)
- » IBM AIX servers
- » F5 load balancers
- » Oracle Databases

There could be many hundreds of instances of the above classes of CIs. You only need to select one instance from each class and manually verify that it is populated correctly in the CMDB. You can then safely assume that the other members of each class are correct.

TIP

After you identify a few instances of CIs in each class, you can assign them to different individuals to verify their accuracy. You've now done a lot of quality assurance on your CMDB with minimal effort!

Building Trust in the Configuration Management Team and the Data

Many processes and people downstream of the CMDB depend on the quality and accuracy of the data in the CMDB to do their jobs. When inaccurate data affects the success of those processes, those people lose trust in the CMDB and the configuration management team. If you're in the unfortunate position of having to rebuild trust, the following guidelines may help:

- » Acknowledge that the process and artifacts are bad, that there is a problem, and that you're going to fix it.
- » Document the steps you're taking to fix the CMDB data. Make sure the steps don't overreach. Set proper expectations

CHAPTER 4 Keeping the Configuration Management Database Healthy and Trusted   39 and overdeliver. This would be a really bad time to overpromise and underdeliver!

» Communicate, communicate, communicate. Provide accurate, honest, and concise communication every step of the way on what has been accomplished and where things stand.

» Establish procedures for identifying and communicating data issues from the user community and a feedback loop for how and when these issues will be addressed.

» Establish a quality control plan and communicate the plan.

» Involve the larger user community in quality control and make the best use of their time.

Measuring Success

Configuration management is an ongoing discipline in any organization. It will always change. The changes come from the evolution of corporate strategies that are then translated into technology decisions that then need to be implemented.

When configuration management is most successful, no one notices that it exists, just like a well-run accounting organization. It's important to regularly measure your effectiveness and benefit to the organization. The configuration management team should collect metrics on the following:

» How many configuration management requests are fulfilled

» CMDB defects identified and fixed

» Number of CIs missing key attributes

» Size of CMDB (only for the classes being managed in the data dictionary)

» Number of incidents and changes placed on items where there is no corresponding CI

» Number of reports designed and run

» List of IT use cases for which the CMDB is being utilized with detailed metrics on each (for example, number and type of reports produced)

Additional metrics should be defined and collected, as appropriate, for your organization's unique requirements. These metrics will help you develop an objective performance scorecard for your configuration management team to identify what's working well, and what opportunities exist for improvement. In this way, you can ensure that your configuration management team and the CMDB remains relevant, trusted, and valuable for your organization regardless of the changes ahead.

Leveraging the CMDB Health Dashboard

When you have the tools and processes in place for a healthy CMDB, you need to keep it healthy and resolve issues as they arise. The best way to do this is to monitor your CMDB using a CMDB dashboard. Using a dashboard (see Figure 4-1), you can monitor key CMDB health key performance indicators (KPIs), including:

» **Completeness:** Test for required and recommended fields that are not populated.

» **Compliance:** Audit the CMDB for its adherence to predefined regulatory requirements, internal governance, and certifications.

» **Correctness:** Test against predefined data integrity rules such as identification rules, orphan CI rules, and stale CI rules.

FIGURE 4-1: Overall CMDB Health dashboard with completeness, compliance, and correctness scorecards.

In addition to aggregate scorecards, you can also drill into CMDB health details for specific business services, groups of CIs, and individual CIs. For example, a CMDB Completeness Health dashboard (see Figure 4-2) may show CIs missing required and recommended attributes, while a CMDB Correctness Health dashboard (see Figure 4-3) may show duplicate and orphan CIs, as well as the overall stale CI trend. This allows you to pinpoint CMDB health problems and request corrective action — for example, by following up with corresponding CI owners or business service owners when CIs become stale.

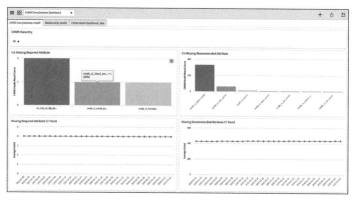

FIGURE 4-2: CMDB Completeness Health dashboard.

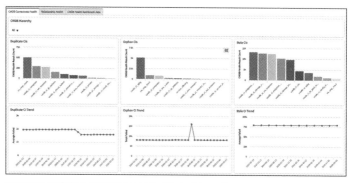

FIGURE 4-3: CMDB Correctness Health dashboard.

> **IN THIS CHAPTER**
>
> » Creating your team and aligning your configuration items
>
> » Choosing appropriate configuration item classes for your use cases
>
> » Ensuring effective communications processes and training
>
> » Automating information flows and enabling continuous improvement
>
> » Expanding capabilities and integrating incident and change management

Chapter **5**

Ten Important Milestones on the Configuration Management Journey

Here are ten milestones to work toward along your organization's journey to successful configuration management:

» You have a configuration management team led by a configuration manager. (See Chapter 1.)

» You have either aligned or are in the process of aligning your configuration items (CIs) to a services-oriented view. (See Chapter 2.)

» The CI classes you've chosen to implement support your stated use cases. (See Chapters 1 and 2.)

- You've invested the necessary time and energy to effectively set up communication processes so that information flows both from the CMDB team to all stakeholders and to the CMDB team from all stakeholders.

- You've made training for all stakeholders a priority and they have a clear sense of your vision and goals.

- To the degree possible, you've automated the flow of information into the CMDB at a frequency that supports your stated use cases.

- You've created a workflow that is designed to audit the integrity and completeness of the data within the CMDB in a manner that leads to continuous improvement.

- All stakeholders understand the importance of the CMDB being the single source of truth for all stated use cases and all supported downstream activities.

- The configuration management team can adequately respond to requests for additional CI classes and expanded use cases.

- The incident and change management processes are continuously improving, with an eye toward impacted services, because a majority of the CIs involved in these processes are available within the CMDB and are being utilized to efficiently manage these workflows.